J 597.3 Hib
Hibbert, Clare
If you were a shark

IF YOU WERE A
SHARK

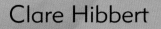

Clare Hibbert

Smart Apple Media

Published in the United States by Smart Apple Media
PO Box 3263, Mankato, Minnesota 56002

Editor: Joe Harris
Picture researcher: Clare Hibbert
Designer: Emma Randall

Picture credits:
All images Shutterstock except unless otherwise specified. Corbis: 7tl. FLPA: 10bl, 11b, 12tl, 12–13 main, 19r, 27b, 15cr, 22b, 12tr, 19t, 27t. Getty: 26–27 main, 29tr. Seapics: 20l, 26l.

Library of Congress Cataloging-in-Publication Data

Hibbert, Clare, 1970-
 If you were a shark / Clare Hibbert.
     p. cm. -- (If you were a--)
 Audience: Grade 4 to 6.
 Summary: "Describes the features, life, and habits of sharks, and contrasts them to human life"--
Provided by publisher.
 Includes bibliographical references and index.
 ISBN 978-1-59920-962-3 (library binding)
 1. Sharks--Juvenile literature. 2. Sharks--Behavior--Juvenile literature. I. Title. II. Title: Shark.
 QL638.9.H53 2014
 597.3--dc23
                                  2013002970

Printed in China

Supplier 03, Date 0513, Print Run 2371
SL002678US

Contents

All Kinds of Sharks

If you were a shark, you might be bigger than a truck or small enough to fit on a person's hand. You might be a harmless giant or a fierce killer. Sharks are a more varied family of creatures than we often imagine.

Shark Appearances

The typical shark is a speedy hunter with a triangular fin on its back and a bullet-shaped body. However, sharks come in many shapes and sizes. Dogfish (shown left) are the most common sharks. They are about 3.3 feet (1 m) long.

Shark Questions

Q: Is it true that sharks never sleep?
A: Yes. Sharks never fall deeply asleep like humans. They keep swimming to move water through their gills. They have "resting times", though, when they let one half of their brain switch off.

How Sharks Breathe

Like all fish, sharks take in oxygen from the water. As a shark swims, it gulps in seawater and pushes it out through gill slits on the sides of its head. Inside the gills, oxygen passes from the water into the shark's bloodstream.

Where Sharks Live

There are around 375 species, or types, of shark. They live in all the world's oceans, from icy polar waters to warm, tropical seas. They also live at all levels of the ocean, from the shallows to the deep.

Shark Teeth

If you were a shark, you would have a set of razor-sharp teeth. They would be the perfect shape for catching and eating your preferred prey, whether it was plankton, shellfish, fish, or dolphins. Your strong jaws and jaw muscles would give you an unbeatable bite.

Rows of Teeth

Sharks' teeth are replaced every couple of weeks, so they are always in peak condition. They are arranged in rows in the mouth. As one tooth or row of teeth falls out, new ones move forward to take their place. Over their lifetime, sharks may get through 20,000 teeth!

Tooth Shapes

Shark teeth come in different shapes to suit their owners' diets. Spearlike teeth are good for catching slippery fish and squid, while blunt teeth can crush shells. Great whites have triangular cutting teeth for slicing into seals.

Shark Questions

Q: Which shark has the biggest jaws?
A: The great white has the largest jaw span. Its bite is twice as strong as a lion's and exerts 15 times more pressure than a human bite can.

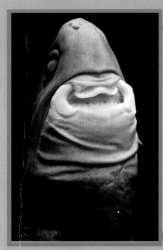

Strange Bite
The cookiecutter shark is named for its unusual feeding method. It bites circular chunks out of larger animals, such as dolphins and whales. The wounds eventually heal, leaving the victims with 2-inch (5-cm) round scars.

Sight and Sound

If you were a shark, your good eyesight and excellent hearing would help you to target prey. In clear water, you could see up to 98 feet (30 m) away. Your hearing would be even more impressive—you could hear certain sounds from 1 mile (1.6 km) away!

Sharks' Eyes

Not all sharks' eyes are the same. Some sharks have color vision, but most see the world in shades of gray. Some kinds have a third eyelid that draws across the eye to protect it when the shark bites. Others simply roll their eyeballs up at the moment of biting.

"Night Vision"

Unlike other fish, sharks can dilate (widen) their pupils to control how much light enters the eye. They can also make the most of the light in dim conditions, thanks to a mirror at the back of the eye, like that in cats' eyes. This gives sharks good vision in murky waters.

Shark Questions

Q: Why are some sharks blind?
A: Most Greenland sharks are blinded by parasites called copepods that fix themselves to the sharks' eyes. However, the copepods produce light that attracts prey, so it doesn't really matter that the sharks can't see!

Shark Hearing

Sharks can pick up low-frequency sounds best, and they are more likely to react to irregular sounds—the kinds of sounds produced by an injured animal thrashing around. Sound is often the first thing that alerts sharks to prey.

Smell, Taste, and Touch

If you were a shark, your senses would give you the edge as a top ocean predator. You would have some unique sensory abilities, as well as sharing the senses that humans have. You would rely a lot on your keen sense of smell.

Sense of Smell

Sharks use smell to find a mate and to navigate, but most of all to track down prey. They show interest in certain smells—such as blood—and totally ignore others. A shark can sniff out an injured animal from more than 1 mile (1.6 km) away.

How Sharks Smell

As a shark swims, seawater flows through its nostrils—the two flaps of skin at the end of its snout—and onto the nasal sacs behind. These sacs have sensory cells that can detect scents and send messages to the shark's brain.

Taste and Touch

Sharks have taste buds all over the inside of their mouth and throat, not just on the tongue. Some sharks also have whiskery feelers called barbels that have taste buds on the ends and which allow them to taste and "feel" prey.

Shark Questions

Q: Can sharks smell better than us?
A: They can't distinguish between as many different smells as we can, but they are very sensitive to certain smells. They can sniff out one drop of blood in a million drops of water!

Supersenses

If you were a shark, you would be equipped with extra-special senses to help you hunt. Your body would be dotted with pressure sensors, and you would also have electrosensory perception—the ability to detect electrical signals in the water.

The Lateral Line

Sharks have a line of sensory cells running along each side of their head and body. Water swishes over these lines of cells as sharks swim, sending signals to their brain about pressure changes and movement in the water.

Reading Ripples

The lateral line allows sharks to build up a clear "picture" of their surroundings—and to notice changes to the usual currents. Sharks can pick up the vibrations produced by a thrashing fish from 328 feet (100 m) away!

The "Sixth Sense"

Sharks have small pits, or openings, around their nose called ampullae of Lorenzini. These can sense electrical signals from about 20 inches (50 cm) away. Moving muscles produce electricity, so this sense helps sharks to target their prey even more precisely.

Shark Questions

Q: Are sharks the only animals that sense electrical signals?
A: No. Their close cousins, rays, have this ability, too, and so do some other aquatic animals, including electric eels, some dolphins, and platypuses.

On the Move

If you were a shark, you would always be hunting. You'd put on short bursts of speed to catch your prey—perhaps even moving as fast as 43 miles per hour (70 km/h). You would need to eat around three percent of your body weight in food each day just to survive.

Designed for Swimming

A typical shark has a streamlined body. Its pointy snout and smooth sides allow it to glide through the sea without using much energy. Most sharks only move forward and must turn around to move toward something behind them.

Shark Questions

Q: What is the shark's top fin for?
A: In scary movies, a dorsal fin poking above the surface warns us that a shark is coming. In reality, the dorsal fin acts like a stabilizer and stops the shark from rolling in the water.

Shark Fins

The flow of water over sharks' pectoral (side) and pelvic (bottom) fins produces lift—just like air flowing over a plane's wing. This stops sharks from sinking. Sharks change direction by tilting their fins.

Skin in Close-up

A shark's skin looks smooth—but if you stroked it the wrong way, it would feel like sandpaper. It is covered by tiny overlapping scales, called denticles, that reduce drag. Throughout the shark's life, old denticles drop off and are replaced by new ones.

Shark Tails

If you were a shark, you'd move your head from side to side as you swam and use your tail to thrust your body through the water. The shape of your tail would be perfectly suited to the kind of swimmer and hunter you were.

Slow Movers

Sharks that spend most of their time on the seabed do not need to use their fins to put on bursts of speed. Nurse sharks' tails have almost no bottom lobe. These sharks sweep their eel-like tails to and fro as they hunt for crabs and lobsters.

Darting and Dodging

The length of the upper lobe affects a shark's ability to maneuver. In tiger sharks, the upper lobe is much longer than the lower one. This asymmetry allows them to twist, turn, and change direction in an instant and also accelerate very quickly.

Sharks' Lobes

Here you can clearly see the upper and lower lobes of a shark's tail. In most fish, the spine stops just before the tail, but sharks are different. Their backbone extends into the upper lobe, giving it extra power.

Shark Questions

Q: What are sharks' skeletons made of?
A: Shark "bones" are not really made of bone at all. Their skeletons are made up of a lighter, more flexible material called cartilage. Humans have cartilage, too, for instance, at the end of the nose.

Man-Eaters

If you were a shark, you would be a fierce predator. You might be one of the dozen or so species that are dangerous to people. If you were a great white, you would have the most fearsome reputation of all and would have even starred in horror movies!

Jaws

The great white's hunting method helps it to kill seals—and sometimes people—without injuring itself. First, it rises up at an angle and takes a surprise bite out of its prey. Then it circles, waiting for blood loss to weaken its victim, before moving in to enjoy its meal.

Swimming Garbage Cans

Tiger sharks attack divers and surfers, partly because they look similar to seals from beneath—and partly because tiger sharks snap up anything and everything! All kinds of odd objects have been found in their stomachs, including car license plates.

Shark Questions

Q: How likely am I to be killed by a shark?
A: There are fewer than 100 shark attacks per year and only 5 to 15 fatalities. You are 250 times more likely to be killed by lightning than by a shark.

Freshwater Menace

Bull sharks swim far up rivers and into lakes, so they are more likely to meet (and eat) swimmers than sharks that stay out at sea. Bull sharks are widespread and found in the Amazon, Zambezi, and Ganges rivers.

Pack Hunters

If you were a shark, you might be a loner—or you might hunt as part of a pack. Perhaps you would simply share the same feeding grounds with many other sharks of the same species. Or perhaps you would cooperate with your pack mates to catch more food.

Working Together

Copper sharks (shown here) and silky sharks cooperate to hunt. They work together to herd fish into a ball shape called a bait ball. Then the sharks start snapping at the closely packed fish.

Easy Targets

Gray nurse sharks work together, too. They thrash their tails to drive fish into the shallows. The action creates underwater waves that sweep the prey toward shore. Reef sharks may follow the nurse sharks to steal a share of the trapped fish.

Feeding Together

Blue sharks are sometimes called the "wolves of the sea". They spend a lot of their time as loners but also form schools, or groups, when they hunt. Blue sharks have a diet of fish, squid, and seabirds.

Shark Question

Q: What's a feeding frenzy?
A: Once a group of sharks finds lots of prey, the blood in the water and the jerky movements of the fish overexcite the sharks. They might lunge at each other as well as the prey!

Filter Feeders

If you were a shark, you might not deserve your scary reputation. You might be one of the gentle giants that filter tiny fish and plankton from the water. Whale sharks (see main image), basking sharks, and megamouths are all filter feeders.

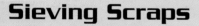

Sieving Scraps

Filter feeders such as this basking shark swim along with their huge mouths wide open. Every so often, they shut their jaws, forcing seawater through the gills. Bristles called gill rakers strain food from the water and channel it into the throat.

Hitching a Ride

Whale sharks don't just feed themselves—they feed hangers-on, too. Remoras are small fish that use suckers on their heads to fix themselves to whale sharks' bellies. They eat scraps that fall from the mouths of their hosts.

Shark Questions

Q: How do sharks lure their food to them?
A: Megamouths are mysterious sharks that live in the deep ocean. They have glow-in-the-dark spots around their mouths that seem to lure plankton and small fish.

Suction Feeding

Whale sharks and megamouths (shown here) are able to vacuum up water and food. Thanks to suction power and a gaping 5-foot- (1.5-m-) wide mouth, a whale shark can take in enough tiny plankton to sustain its 15-ton bulk.

Migration

If you were a shark, you might travel long distances in search of feeding grounds or a mate. If you were a great white (see main image), for example, you might make regular ocean crossings. Your supersenses would help you to navigate by detecting changes in the surrounding water.

Atlantic Migrants

Female blue sharks feed and mate off the east coast of North America, then travel across the Atlantic to give birth off the coast of Africa. The round trip, which they make every three years or so, is 9,500 miles (15,000 km).

Feeding Grounds

Tiger sharks travel to take advantage of gluts of easy prey. The sharks arrive in the waters around Hawaii just as the albatross chicks hatch, then continue onward to eastern Australia in time for the turtle season.

Shark Questions

Q: How do sharks find their way?
A: Their electrosensory perception (see page 12) helps them to use the Earth's magnetism like an inbuilt compass.

Freshwater Nurseries
Bull sharks migrate along freshwater rivers (see page 19) to have their young. Some have been found as far as 2,600 miles (4,200 km) up the Amazon! No other sharks can survive such long periods in fresh water.

Shark Babies

If you were a shark, you might have started life in one of three ways. Your mother might have given birth to you, or you might have hatched from an egg—either inside your mother or in the sea. You probably spent your early years in safe, sheltered waters.

Viviparity (Live Young)

Lemon sharks are one of the few shark species that give birth to live young. Their litters can contain up to 17 pups. The pups develop inside their mother, and an umbilical cord brings them oxygen and nutrients from the placenta.

Shark Questions

Q: Do shark moms look after their babies?
A: Shark mothers abandon their babies, but they do give them a good start in life. They have their pups in shallow, coastal waters, where they will be safe for their early years.

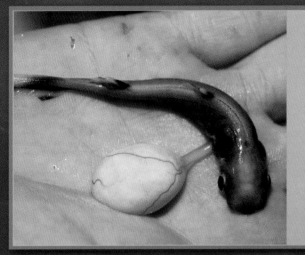

Ovoviviparity (Inner Hatching)

Most sharks develop inside eggs inside their mother's body, not connected to her by an umbilical cord or placenta. When they are fully developed, the babies "hatch" and are born. Sometimes the newborn pups are still attached to their yolk sac, which provides them with food.

Oviparity (Outside Hatching)

About a third of sharks lay eggs into the water. The egg cases harden in the water and protect the growing embryo for six to 12 months. Then, the pup swims out of the case. Washed-up cases are nicknamed "mermaids' purses".

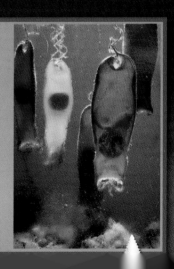

A Very Strange Family

If you were a shark, you might not fit the mold. Unlike the typical members of your family, you might not have a sleek, streamlined body or a pointed dorsal fin. You might have a flattened body, a weird head, or an unusual snout. You might be one of the oddballs.

Wide-Eyed Weirdos

Hammerhead sharks have wide, hammer-shaped heads with eyes on the tips. Swinging their heads from side to side gives them superb all-around vision. Hammerheads often gather in their hundreds to rest by day.

Long and Lethal Weapon

Saw sharks are extremely rare. They have wide, flat bodies, but their distinguishing feature is a long, narrow snout, studded with pointy teeth. The sharks use this "saw" to slash at fish or to probe the seabed for shellfish.

Shark Questions

Q: Were there sharks in dinosaur times?
A: Yes—and long before then, too. Ancestors of the shark were swimming in the world's oceans 450 million years ago, 220 million years before the first dinosaurs appeared.

Carpet Sharks

Some sharks have mottled markings that look like carpet patterns and help to camouflage them. The tasseled wobbegong is one of the strangest carpet sharks. Its seaweedlike tentacles swish in the current, disguising the shark and attracting prey.

Glossary

ampullae of Lorenzini Jelly-filled pits around a shark's nose that allow it to detect electrical signals.

ancestor A member of the family that lived long ago.

aquatic Describes something from the water.

asymmetry Not being symmetrical (not having both halves exactly the same).

bait ball A mass of fish prey that has been herded together into a ball.

barbel One of a pair of whiskery feelers found on some sharks' noses.

camouflage To make something blend in to the surroundings so it is hard to spot.

cartilage The light, flexible material from which a shark's skeleton is made.

cooperate Work together to achieve a shared aim.

copepod A small crustacean (animal with a hard shell).

denticle A small scale on a shark's skin.

dorsal fin The fin on a shark's back, between its head and its tail fin.

drag A force that slows down movement through the water or the air.

electrosensory perception The ability to sense electrical signals given out by other animals.

embryo A developing young animal before it has hatched or been born.

feeding frenzy An aggressive attack on prey by a group of overexcited sharks.

filter feeder A shark that uses gill rakers to strain plankton and small fish from the water.

gill A slit on the side of a fish's head used for breathing.

gill raker A bristly, comblike part of the gills, used to filter food from the water.

lateral line A line of jelly-filled pores that runs along each side of a shark's body and helps it to sense tiny vibrations and movements in the water.

migration The regular, usually seasonal, movement of animals from one place to another in search of food or a mate, or to give birth.

navigate To find the way.

oviparity A method of reproduction where the mother lays eggs.

ovoviviparity A method of reproduction where eggs develop and hatch inside the mother's body.

parasite An animal that lives on another animal and relies on it for food.

pectoral fin One of a pair of fins on a shark's sides that are behind the head.

pelvic fin One of a pair of fins on a shark's sides between the stomach and tail.

placenta A large organ that forms inside the pregnant females of some species, which supports the developing embryo by providing oxygen and food along the umbilical cord.

plankton Tiny animals and plants, often microscopic, that float near the surface of the ocean.

prey An animal that is hunted by other animals for food. Small fish are typical prey for sharks.

taste buds Parts of the mouth that send signals to the brain, which then makes sense of that information, allowing an animal to taste.

Further Reading

100 Facts on Sharks by Steve Parker (Miles Kelly Publishing, 2010)

Kingfisher Knowledge: Sharks by Miranda Smith (Kingfisher, 2008)

National Geographic Kids Everything Sharks by Ruth Musgrave (National Geographic Children's Books, 2011)

Sharkpedia by Nancy Ellwood and Margaret Parrish (Dorling Kindersley, 2008)

Sharks (Insiders) by Beverly McMillan (Simon & Schuster Books for Young Readers, 2008)

Web Sites

http://animals.nationalgeographic.com/animals/fish/great-white-shark/
Information on great whites from National Geographic.

dsc.discovery.com/tv/shark-week/
Discovery Channel's Shark Week web site.

www.flmnh.ufl.edu/fish/sharks/isaf/isaf.htm
The International Shark Attack File's official web site.

http://www.sharks.org
The Shark Research Institute, a web site dedicated to shark awareness and protection.

www.oceana.org
The web site for Oceana, a worldwide organization dedicated to ocean conservation and the protection of marine habitats and endangered species.

Index